How to
in a Few Months
While Enjoying Yourself

45 Proven Tips

for Language Learners

By Nate Nicholson

Subscribe to My Newsletter

Sign up for my newsletter at http://eepurl.com/bb8sQ9 to get a bonus chapter listing my favorite language learning sites. It's available both in a .mobi file you can send to your Kindle and in a .pdf file.

You'll also get exclusive updates about my new titles. Subscribers of my newsletter who are willing to write reviews have the opportunity to get free advance reader copies of my new books.

Don't worry – I don't send emails more often than once per week (and usually less often than that).

CONTENTS

Subscribe to My Newsletter 2

Introduction 4

Chapter 1: Proper Mindset
to Learn a Language Quickly 6

Chapter 2: Speaking Skills 9

Chapter 3: Listening Skills 21

Chapter 4: Reading Skills 30

Chapter 5: Writing Skills 37

Chapter 6: Additional Tips and Tricks
to Improve Your Language Skills 44

Chapter 7: Nine Common Mistakes to Avoid ... 55

Chapter 8: Five Common Challenges 68

Afterword 76

Subscribe to My Newsletter 78

Support the Author 79

Books by Nate Nicholson 80

Introduction

Everyone can become fluent in a foreign language in a matter of a few months. The key, however, is to understand fluency as the ability to communicate with native speakers with relative ease, not as being 100% accurate.

Perfectionism is one of the most common obstacles for language learners who believe that if they can't speak 100% correctly, they shouldn't start learning a foreign language at all.

When you let go of the belief that fluency is 100% accuracy all the time, you will stop wasting time learning things that won't lead you to fluency. You will focus on the most important things. Moreover, you will stop being so afraid of making mistakes. Consequently, you too will be able to become a fluent speaker of a foreign language in a few months.

I know it from personal experience. I taught myself Spanish in a mere few months. But here's the key – I focused on what was useful to me, not on becoming perfect.

My definition of fluency is if you can talk with native speakers of your target language about the usual topics you like talking about in your native language, you're fluent. I don't have the ability to talk about astrophysics in English, so why should I demand from myself to know how to do it in Spanish, French, Italian or any other language I want to learn?

A few months after I started learning, I could have one-hour conversations with native speakers. Did I make mistakes? Sure. Did the native speakers still understand me? Absolutely. I was fluent by my definition. If you dropped me into the middle of a Spanish-speaking country, I would get by just fine.

In this book, I would like to share with you some of my most effective language learning techniques so that you too can achieve fluency in a few months. Consider each of these methods a building block to your success in learning a new language.

Chapter 1: Proper Mindset to Learn a Language Quickly

Before I share with you the most effective tips to become fluent in a language in a few months, we need to talk about the fundamentals – your mindset.

Here are three important things you have to understand before we talk about improving your language skills.

#1: Believe It's Possible

Your mindset will have a huge influence on your results. If you believe it takes a few years to learn a language, it will take you a few years to learn it. If you believe it's possible to become fluent in under a year, you will do it in under a year.

Don't make excuses as to why you can't learn a language quickly. You're never too old to learn a new language. You don't need to travel to learn a language (it can help, but you don't need it). You don't need to have a teacher to become fluent (it can help, but it isn't necessary).

When you instill in yourself the belief that you can do it, obstacles won't set you back. You can achieve much more than you think, but only if you don't limit yourself.

#2: Have a Strong Why

A strong reason why you want to learn a foreign language will help you stick to your routine when the going gets tough.

Before you embark on your journey to learn another language, find a powerful motivation why you want to do it. Is it because you want to have more work opportunities? Do you want to learn the language of your grandparents? Do you love the culture of the country whose language you want to learn?

No matter what your "why" is it has to be strong enough to fire you up and keep you going when you feel frustrated. It's much easier to learn a language when you have a good reason to do it.

#3: Don't Try to Be Perfect, Just Get It Going

Jack Canfield once said, "You don't have to get it perfect, you just have to get it going. Babies don't walk the first time they try, but eventually they get it right."

It's the same with learning languages. Perfectionism will hold you back. There are many people who understand the technical aspects of a language they're learning, but they never speak it because they don't want to make a mistake.

Each mistake you make is an opportunity to learn something new. It's fine to make embarrassing mistakes, sound ridiculous, or use broken sentences. We all have to do it before we master the language we're studying. The sooner you accept this fact, the sooner you will make progress.

Chapter 2: Speaking Skills

If I were to rate language skills in the order of importance, I would give first place to speaking and listening skills.

I became fluent in Spanish in a few months, but not because I spent hours and hours reading and writing. I learned it quickly because I made it my priority to understand the spoken language. I put emphasis on interacting with native speakers and content presented in its natural real-world form.

As a result, I wasn't startled when I traveled to Mexico and had to do everything in Spanish on a daily basis (I made a promise to myself to not use English at all).

I wasn't surprised because I didn't spend time with handbooks, simple audios for language learners, and so on. By the time I went to Mexico, I had already listened to the real-world spoken Mexican Spanish for countless hours.

If you want to learn a language quickly, there's no other way to do it than by speaking with natives as soon as possible. It's scary, it's uncomfortable, but it's the most effective way to improve your skills quickly.

In this chapter, I will give you five powerful tips to improve your speaking skills even when you've only just started learning a new language.

#1: Use Language Exchange Sites

Language exchange sites make it extremely easy to find a native speaker willing to help you learn his or her mother language in exchange for teaching him or her English.

Some of the most popular language exchange sites (I list them in the bonus chapter) include Livemocha.com, MyLanguageExchange.com, and Interpals.com.

When you join one of these sites, make sure to fill out your profile, and pick the language you speak and the language you want to learn. Then use the search feature to find a potential pen pal.

Send a short and sweet message to encourage people to reply to you. You can write something like this (of course, in your target language):

Hi [first name],

My name is John. I'm from New York City. I'd love to help you learn English in exchange for the opportunity to learn Spanish from you.

Would you be interested in a language exchange?

Best,

John

Keep in mind that many users won't reply to you, as a lot of people create an account, visit the site once and never come back. It may take much more than just a few messages to find someone who will reply to you (it took me at least 20 messages to find my pen pal). Keep sending messages, and sooner or later someone will reply to you.

I admit there's a bit of a weirdness factor when talking to a stranger you've met online. Moreover, I noticed that many men on these sites consider them dating sites. Avoid sending messages to people who have any sexual innuendos in their profile (or virtually anything related to dating, such as, "I'm lonely").

If you're a woman, I recommend sending messages to other women, only. This way, you will avoid a lot of creeps.

If you're a guy, I still recommend sending messages to women. I tried sending messages to men and almost none of them replied to me (perhaps because I'm not a sexy blonde). Sending messages to women was more effective.

Keep your messages polite and avoid any innuendos (and don't comment on appearances). You're there to learn a language, not date. That's how I met my female pen pal.

Once you break the ice, it's one of the most effective ways to improve your language skills and learn the language in its most natural form.

There's a wide variety of programs to video chat, but the most popular one you're probably going to use is Skype.

Once you schedule your conversation, prepare some basic sentences you can say about yourself. After exchanging pleasantries and getting to know basic facts about each other, establish how you're going to teach each other. You can either devote one full session to speaking in a foreign language and another to speaking in English or divide each session into two parts.

Please keep in mind that the less often you use English when speaking with your pen pal, the more quickly you will learn. Consequently, I don't recommend switching from one language to another when you're saying something in the language you're studying.

When you're in Spanish mode (or whatever language you're learning), stick to Spanish, no matter how hard it is to explain something. When you're in teaching mode, speak your native language to force your pen pal to improve his or her listening skills.

#2: Talk to Your Pet (or Yourself)

I hope I didn't lose you when you read this subheading. I'm serious, though.

When you practice your speaking skills at home, with nobody to judge you, you can be free to try different things. You can work on your accent without being afraid you sound ridiculous. You can say whatever you want, even if it's nonsense.

A lot of problems with speaking in a foreign language aren't related to the language in itself but to our inner barriers. By getting used to speaking in another language without any other people, it will be easier for you to open up when they are around.

#3: Host Native Speakers at Your Home

If you have an empty bed, or better yet, an empty room in your house, consider creating an account on Couchsurfing.org and hosting strangers at your home. It's a site that connects travelers with people who are willing to offer them free accommodation (usually for a few days at most).

The idea of the site may sound ridiculous or scary (hosting strangers in your home?), but fortunately, it's extremely rare to encounter any dangerous people on this site.

First and foremost, there's a system of reviews to ensure that you're hosting nice people. You aren't obliged to host people with no reviews. In fact, you aren't obliged to host anyone. If you don't like the profile of the person who sent you the request, you can decline it. If someone has a few reviews (a few people who vouched for him or her), he or she is probably a trustworthy person.

Secondly, nobody forces you to leave your guests unattended. You can only host people on the weekends when you don't have work and can spend time with them. Some hosts give keys to the house to their guests, some don't. It's your choice.

Last but not least, Couchsurfing offers its users an option to verify their identity. To stay on the safe side, you can decline requests from people who haven't verified their identity.

If you live in a place popular among tourists, you may get a request every week or so (or even more often). If you live in a less popular place, you will still receive requests from time, but probably only once every few weeks or months.

Of course, there's no guarantee that by offering a couch on Couchsurfing only native speakers of your target language will request to stay at your place. However, if you like the idea of the site, it's still a good way to create new opportunities to interact with native speakers. A few days spent exploring your city with native speakers would greatly improve your skills.

#4: Meet with Native Speakers in Your City

There are numerous sites where you can find people sharing common interests. On many of these sites, you can find groups for expats, language learners or people interested in the culture of a country whose language you're learning. In other words, groups with native speakers of your target language.

Meetup.com is one of the best such sites. Browse through local groups and find the ones with native speakers of your target language. Attend their meetings to get to know native speakers living in your city.

It's completely free, and provides an excellent opportunity to immerse yourself in another language without traveling. It's also much safer than meeting with an individual from Craigslist – Meetup.com is for groups of people.

#5: Travel

Spending time in a foreign country is one of the most powerful ways to immerse yourself in its culture and learn its language extremely quickly. Even just a few days spent in another country can tremendously help you improve your language skills.

Traveling doesn't have to be as expensive as you think, especially if you're learning the language of the neighboring country. There are numerous cheap flights and ways to get affordable accommodation (or even free if you choose to stay with a couchsurfer).

There's an important thing you have to remember to make the most out of traveling – English (or whatever languages you already speak) is forbidden. If you're traveling to Mexico, speak only Spanish. Some native speakers will switch to English to help you understand them. Reply to them in Spanish, anyway. It will send a clear message that you're serious about learning their language – and they will appreciate it.

Struggling while speaking is a frustrating but necessary part of the process. If you don't venture outside your comfort zone and keep using English for learning purposes, you may as well stay at home. Traveling gives you an opportunity to surround yourself with your target language. Don't lose this opportunity by sticking to what is easy.

Before you go on your trip, make sure to learn some of the most common phrases and sentences you will use in everyday situations. Don't forget to learn other useful phrases for conversational purposes such as, "Let me think about it for a second", "Could you repeat it?", "I don't understand," or, "It's an interesting question."

When listening to a native speaker, try to get the gist of what he or she said and deduct everything else from the context. People all over the world ask the same kind of questions in everyday situations.

For instance, if you're shopping and the cashier told you something about the card, he probably asked you if you want to pay with your credit card or use cash. If you aren't sure, ask the cashier to repeat what he said, or ask him if you understood him correctly.

Most people will be patient with a person who's learning their native language, especially if you're in a place where most tourists don't bother to learn even the most common words. The key is to always have a smile on your face and be respectful.

Last but not least, don't forget about the universal language understood all over the world – body language. If you don't know how to say something, you can explain it with your hands or point to it. When you let go of your reservations, you can have a lot of fun trying to explain something to a speaker of another language.

Traveling is one of the most effective ways to learn a language, but it doesn't mean it's the only way to learn a language quickly. You can create a similar language "bubble" at your home by meeting with native speakers on a regular basis, talking, chatting or exchanging emails with pen pals, watching movies and listening to podcasts and music in your target language. It takes more effort, but it can still be done.

Traveling facilitates this process, as when you're in a foreign country, everything around you is already in another language. When you're determined, though, nothing prevents you from creating a pretty similar experience while never leaving your home.

Summing It Up

The only way to improve your speaking skills is to speak as much as possible. No amount of reading, writing or listening will replace the real-world practice of talking with other people. Find ways to speak with native speakers and do it on a regular basis.

The sooner you will start speaking, the more quickly you will master a new language. It's the most uncomfortable, but also the most important step you have to take on your journey toward fluency.

Chapter 3: Listening Skills

There are two types of listening: active listening and passive listening. Active listening is when you listen to something and pay attention to it. Passive listening is listening to something in the background.

Active listening will help you develop your listening skills, while passive listening is largely a waste of time.

In this chapter, I'll cover my five most effective ways to improve your listening skills. By using these methods on a daily basis, you will train your ear to understand your target language the way it's spoken. Even if you don't understand everything a native speaker is saying, you will be able to get the gist of it and follow what's being said.

#1: Watch Movies without Subtitles

Watching movies, and especially TV series without subtitles, is hands down one of the best methods to learn a new language. I spent countless hours watching great Spanish movies and TV series. In fact, one of the TV series I watched is now one of my favorite TV series of all time, and it was never available in English. Just another perk of speaking more than one language.

The key here is the same as with books – watch what you enjoy watching in your native language.

Finding titles of good movies in your target language may be a bit tricky if you don't know my simple hack. Here it is step by step:

1. Go to IMDB.com Advanced Title Search: http://www.imdb.com/search/title

2. Check the title type that interests you (for instance, "TV Series").

3. Limit the release date to titles released in the last 10 or 20 years or so, unless you enjoy watching older movies. I prefer newer movies as they are of a better quality and are a bit easier to understand.

4. Pick user rating. I like to go with at least 7.0. This way, I know that the movies on the list are good. Everything above 6.0 should be at least okay.

5. Enter the number of votes. To make sure that you'll find good titles, search for something with at

least 100 or so votes (make it a little lower for less popular languages).

6. Pick your genre. Leave it as it is if you aren't searching for a specific genre.

7. Skip everything until you get to "Countries". Here, choose a country whose language you want to learn. If you're learning Spanish, pick the country whose dialect you want to learn, e.g. Mexico for Mexican Spanish and Spain for Castilian Spanish.

8. Pick the language you're learning.

9. Scroll down and click "search". Now you should have a list of good movies or TV series in your target language.

10. Search for these movies online. They may be available on Amazon, Netflix, or on YouTube.

Don't watch these movies with subtitles. Subtitles make you lazy. When you read subtitles, you don't improve your listening skills, because you don't have to – everything is on the screen. When you don't have subtitles, if you want to follow the movie, you have to listen closely. And that's precisely the goal of this method.

If you're watching a movie in a foreign language for the first time, prepare to be frustrated. The first few movies may be difficult to understand, but you'll find yourself quickly getting used to the way the language is spoken. Sooner or later, you will be able to follow the movie with relative ease.

I can't emphasize how important this one tip is. If you can't afford or don't want to speak with native speakers, watching as many movies as possible is a must. It's one of the best ways to learn new vocabulary, get used to the spoken language, improve your accent, and learn the most common phrases and slang.

#2: Listen to Music

Listening to music is less effective than watching movies, but it's still worth a try. What do you like to listen to in your native language? Find it in your target language.

You can use Wikipedia in a language you're learning to find artists performing your favorite genres. The longer the description of the artist is, the more popular he or she usually is.

You can also find them on YouTube by typing the name of your favorite genre along with the word for your language, say, "rock en español."

When listening to music in your target language, don't just play it in the background. Listen to it actively. If you have problems following the song, find lyrics and read them along with the song. Heck, you can even sing along if you want. It's a good way to practice your listening, reading, and speaking skills at the same time.

If you can bear it, record yourself while singing alone. Compare your accent to the accent of the singer. What makes yours different? Do you make pronunciation mistakes? Is your intonation off? What makes a native speaker have a vibe different from yours?

#3: Watch Videos on YouTube

YouTube is a goldmine of videos in virtually every language in the world. I've spent many hours watching old cartoons on YouTube. I found watching them both fun and useful to improve my listening skills as well as my vocabulary.

Since they're aimed at children or teenagers, there's no difficult vocabulary, and they're fairly simple. Moreover, each episode isn't usually longer than 30 minutes or so, which is another bonus when I don't have time to watch an entire 90-minute or 2-hour long movie.

You can use YouTube to find a wide variety of videos in your target language. You can find documentaries, old movies, interviews, cartoons, advertisements, music videos – everything you want to entertain yourself and learn something new in another language.

Subscribe to your favorite channels and watch their new uploads on a daily basis. It's a great way to get immersed in a foreign language and watch something interesting or useful at the same time.

#4: Listen to Podcasts

If you enjoy listening to podcasts, get your daily fix with podcasts in a foreign language.

However, instead of listening to podcasts for language learners, focus on podcasts for regular native speakers of your target language. The reason is simple – podcasts for language learners feature a watered down version of a foreign language. Speakers may speak extremely slowly and in an unnatural way.

When you start with these podcasts and then move on to the regular ones, you will be surprised how much more difficult they are. For this reason, I believe it's better to start with regular podcasts, ideally with podcasts for children or teenagers. They will be easier to understand, but will still feature the language the way it's spoken.

You can look for podcasts either by using Google or by simply heading over to iTunes and looking for podcasts in your target language. With the number of podcasts out there, it's extremely easy to find a podcast about a topic that interests you.

Listening to podcasts is an effective way to improve your language skills during little pockets of time when you have nothing else to do. You can listen to podcasts when commuting, waiting in a line, when taking a walk, and so on. Even if you don't have a lot of free time, you can always find at least 15 minutes per day to listen to a short podcast.

Some podcasts offer free transcriptions of each episode. If you've found a podcast with transcriptions, it's a good idea to listen to it while following the transcription – at least in the beginning when you still don't understand much. Don't use it as a crutch later when you have the ability to listen and understand what's being said without having to read the text.

#5: Listen to the Radio

If you don't enjoy podcasts, you can always listen to the radio. Many radio stations broadcast online. You can use Google to find them by typing "online radio" in your target language in Google for your target country.

Just remember what I mentioned in the beginning of this chapter. Listen actively; don't just leave the radio in the background. You aren't going to learn much if you don't focus on what's being said.

Summing It Up

Your listening skills affect your speaking skills. The more you listen, the easier it will be for you to understand the real-world spoken language and have a regular conversation in it.

Listening skills are one of the easiest skills to develop because you can practice them almost anywhere and at any time. Make use of small pockets of time. Listen to audio files in your target language in your car, when exercising, while waiting, and so on. The more practice you get, the more you'll understand the spoken language.

Chapter 4: Reading Skills

Reading is one of the most pleasurable and effective ways to learn new vocabulary. Instead of memorizing words from boring word lists, you can simply read as much as possible and check the words you don't understand.

Don't try to memorize new words by repeating them every single day, though. Just check the word and try to remember it. Perhaps you'll have to check the same word again the next time you encounter it. Maybe the third time, too. But then after being exposed to it a few times, you'll learn it naturally – just like you learned new words as a child.

In this chapter, I'll cover five techniques to improve your reading skills, learn new vocabulary, and improve your grammar, all at the same time.

#1: Read Children's Stories

In order to learn effectively while reading in a foreign language, it shouldn't be so difficult to understand the text that you have to check every word.

Consequently, I recommend starting with children's stories, or virtually everything in a foreign language written for children – fairy tales, short stories, even non-fiction.

By starting with something simple, you'll avoid a lot of frustration and get a nice boost of self-esteem when you read the entire book and understand it (instead of swearing after finishing each sentence).

When you no longer find children's stories challenging, switch to something more difficult, ideally another real-world text, not a boring article from your handbook. Below are four ideas on what to read when you're done with books for children.

#2: Read Comics

Comics are a wonderful source to improve your reading skills in a fun way. Since there's much less text in a comic than in a book, you won't find yourself checking every word. Moreover, comics are image-based. Images will tremendously help you decipher the dialogue without the need to check every single word.

To make the transition to comics easier, you can start with comics for teenagers. Titles for the adult audience may have much more difficult words than comics primarily aimed at younger people.

You can find comics in foreign languages on Amazon. A simple Google search will also help you find comics in another language (just write something like "comics online" in your target language). Make sure to use Google for your target language, for instance Google.mx for Mexican Spanish.

#3: Read Blogs

Reading blogs is one of my favorite ways to improve my reading skills for two reasons.

Firstly, I can read about something that interests me, thus making learning a new language an interesting activity, not a chore. By reading in a foreign language about things that interest me, I improve my ability to talk about these topics in my target language. Consequently, it's a fast track to fluency.

Secondly, I can learn my target language the way it's spoken by regular people. The vast majority of blogs are written in a conversational tone. Moreover, I can read comments under each article, which is another good way to learn the language the way people use it.

The word "blog" is pretty much universal across the world. If you want to find blogs in your target language about a topic that interests you, type in Google something like "business blogs", for instance "blogs de negocios" in Spanish (use Google in your target language to get better results).

#4: Read News Sites

If you're reading news on a daily basis in your native language, why not switch over to your target language? It's a great way to improve your reading skills and be up to date with what's happening in the world.

By reading news sites in a foreign language, you will also learn about the most common topics in countries that speak your target language. This practice can give you an additional understanding of the culture of the country whose language you're learning.

As with blogs, finding news sites in a foreign language is easy – just type "news" in Google in your target language.

#5: Read Books

The most effective, albeit sometimes frustrating, way to improve your reading skills is to read books. As I mentioned in the beginning of this chapter, I suggest starting with something easier, for instance children's books. When you can understand them without any major problems, you can move on to young adult books, and then to regular books.

When looking for books to read in your target language, follow a simple rule – read what you read in your native language. Don't force yourself to read classic literature if you don't read it in your native language.

Secondly, start with shorter books. They are usually less complex, and should be easier to understand.

Thirdly, if you don't have a rich vocabulary, stick to non-fiction books. Fiction books usually contain a lot of descriptions, frequently with words that aren't used that often in everyday life.

Last but not least, I highly recommend reading books on your Kindle or in Kindle for PC. Kindle has an in-built dictionary for several languages, so if your target language is on the list, you will be able to check each word by highlighting it.

Don't stress over understanding every single word, though. If you keep checking words in every sentence, it's going to be a painstaking process instead of an enjoyable one. If you can't read the book without checking every other word, it's probably too difficult for you, anyway. You don't have to check every word if you probably understand the general meaning.

Summing It Up

You develop your reading skills by reading as much as possible. Don't spend your time with boring articles from textbooks, though. Learn how to read by doing it as a child.

A child learning his language doesn't start with academic books or articles about the process of manufacturing oil. A child starts with simple and short fairy tales. Then he progressively moves to more and more difficult books and keeps expanding his vocabulary.

Follow the same process. Don't feel stupid because you're reading a fairy tale. We all have to start with something, and so it happens that the easiest content is children's stories.

Chapter 5: Writing Skills

Writing and grammar go together. Instead of memorizing boring and extremely difficult to understand grammar rules, spend your time reading and writing a lot. It's the way native speakers learn, and it's the way you should improve your skills, too.

Learning grammar rules without any reference to the real world is like learning how to play the guitar without actually playing it. It just doesn't work. Improving your grammar skills is a much more pleasant and effective activity when you combine it with the five techniques I'm about to share with you in this chapter. For maximum results, don't forget about reading a lot.

#1: Use Online Chats

Online chats for language learners are a great way to find a pen pal, a person who wants to learn your native language instead of teaching you his or her mother tongue. Chatting will help you learn how to write the way native speakers do.

You will learn slang and common phrases in your target language. You will also learn the peculiarities of a language you wouldn't be able to learn from a handbook like writing "haha" in Spanish as "jaja." These are things you aren't going to learn from a book – you can only learn them from a native speaker.

Chatting is a much less uncomfortable way of learning another language than talking on Skype. You have time to check the words you don't understand. You also have a minute or two to check your reply before sending it.

You can start chatting with native speakers even if you started learning a new language just a few days before. How do you do it? Just use Google Translate to translate your sentences to your target language while paying attention to the structure of the sentence and the words. It won't be perfect, but it will still help you a lot – and definitely much more than trying to learn the grammar rules.

One of the most popular language exchange sites with an online chat is Sharedtalk.com. It's available for free. You can go there and search for a native speaker of your target language who's learning English (or whatever your native language is) and hop on a text chat with him or her.

#2: Write in a Journal

Journaling is another activity you can do on a daily basis to improve your writing skills. Even if you write only a few sentences a day, it will still help you learn new words, grammar structures and get you more used to the idea of writing in another language.

You can use free Lang-8.com as your journal. Native speakers of your target language will proofread your entries. In exchange, spend some time helping other users learn English. It's a great way to learn from your own mistakes and get valuable feedback from native speakers.

#3: Check Your Writing with Google

Google is a wonderful teacher. Whenever you're writing something and you aren't sure if you wrote it correctly, you can copy and paste your sentence into Google to check if other people wrote it online. Don't forget to use quotation marks and use Google in your target language.

If there are only a few results, you probably didn't write a given sentence correctly. If there are hundreds or thousands of results, you probably didn't make a mistake.

For better accuracy, you can use Google Books search instead of using regular Google. Google Books searches for your query in printed books, while regular Google searches through content available online.

If something was printed this way, it was probably spelled correctly. With regular Google search there's a possibility you will find a few results written by a non-native speaker or written by a native speaker who made a mistake. Consequently, it's best to stick to Google Books search.

#4: Participate in Online Forums

No matter what hobbies you have, you can find an online forum about them. Again, use our favorite friend – Google. Find the word for your hobby in another language (say "ciclismo" for biking in

Spanish) and type it in Google in your target language along with the word for "forum" or "discussion board."

For instance, if you want to find a Spanish discussion board about biking, you can type "ciclismo foro," or more correctly, "foro de ciclismo."

Join forums that interest you and start participating. You will achieve four things at the same time: improve your reading skills, practice your writing skills, discuss something that interests you and possibly make friends with native speakers of your target language.

Many forums have a separate section for introductions. You can introduce yourself there and tell other people that you're learning their language. Many people are happy to help foreigners learn their language. They will respect you for your efforts and offer you support.

#5: Comment on Blogs

Blogs are great not only as a reading practice, but also as a way to improve your writing skills – leave comments under articles.

Even if you only leave short comments, you will still learn useful things. You can write, "Thank you for writing this post. Sorry for any mistakes – I'm learning your language."

As with forums, it's a wonderful way to have fun while improving your writing skills. You will learn how to ask questions, share your opinion about something or maybe even make a friend or two if you become a regular commenter.

Summing It Up

Learning how to write in your target language by doing it is the best way to improve your vocabulary and learn real-world grammar.

You can always go back to grammar and learn all the rules later when you have some experience with the real-world language. It's a much better approach than learning grammar when you know virtually nothing about your target language and all the examples don't mean anything to you.

Learning grammar can become a fun activity when you combine it with writing something that interests you. You will learn in a much more effective way by using what you have learned straight away.

For instance, instead of memorizing how to write something in the past tense, you can use the past tense every day by writing in your journal. Instead of learning how to use the future tense, you can leave a comment on a blog saying that you will follow the advice.

Chapter 6: Additional Tips and Tricks to Improve Your Language Skills

There are many things you can do to speed up your learning rate, some of them not necessarily related just to learning the language.

In this chapter, I'd like to share with you some of my most powerful tips to learn a new language effectively. When you combine these tips with the advice I shared with you in the previous chapters, you'll be able to become fluent in a new language even in three to six months.

#1: Focus on the Key 20%

The 80/20 Principle says that 80% of the results come from 20% of your efforts. This principle can be also applied to languages.

In vocabulary, learning the 1000 most common words (which is just 1-2% of the entire vocabulary of a language) will help you understand at least 50% of what is being said in everyday situations. You can find frequency lists on Wikipedia here: http://en.wiktionary.org/wiki/Wiktionary:Frequency_l ists.

The 80/20 Principle can be also applied to other aspects of the language. For instance, grammar isn't nearly as important as your ability to pronounce the words correctly. If you say something with broken grammar, people will still understand you. If you say it using completely wrong vowels, it may be much harder to decipher what you're trying to say.

When learning a new language, always ask yourself what is going to be useful to you. For instance, if you don't plan to travel, it doesn't make sense to learn vocabulary related to giving or asking for directions. You can always learn it later on, before your trip.

The 80/20 Principle will ensure that you stop wasting time on the things you aren't going to use. Thanks to this, you will learn much more quickly than a regular person learning things she isn't going to use in the foreseeable future.

#2: Immerse Yourself

Have you ever thought why people who attend language schools have to take classes for years before they're able to communicate in a foreign language? The answer is simple – they only use the language two times per week during their one-hour classes. How are you supposed to learn a language quickly if you only use it for two hours a week? Yet, that's what most people recommend.

Don't follow the conventional path. The fastest way to fluency starts with immersing yourself in your target language. When you surround yourself with it, whether in the form of books, blogs, movies, music, podcasts, and so on, you will make it a part of your life.

Now, instead of studying only two hours per week, you will practice two hours per day. Who's going to learn a language more quickly, all things being equal?

In addition to the methods I already shared with you, there are a couple more ways to immerse yourself in your target language.

The first one is to switch the language of your browser and any other programs to your target language. It's a simple change that will help you learn some new words and use your target language every time you're going to use your computer.

Switch the language of all your online accounts. Change the interface of your e-mail account and profiles on social media.

Change the language on your phone. In fact, if you're using your phone more often than your computer, you should change it before changing anything else.

If you enjoy playing video games, change their language to your target language, too. Do the same with any apps you use.

Write notes, shopping lists, and such in your target language. It's a super easy way to learn the words for the most common items you buy at the store.

If you use social media sites on a daily basis, follow the accounts of native speakers of your target language.

Label items in your house with a piece of tape and the word for the item in your target language. For instance, if you're learning Spanish, label your fridge with "la nevera" or your window with "la ventana." It's a simple way to learn vocabulary related to household items by just walking around your house.

By surrounding yourself with your target language on a daily basis, you will learn it much more quickly than a person who only has contact with it when she's having a lesson. Make it a part of your life, and you will memorize it forever.

#3: Get a List of Cognates

Cognates are words that have a common etymology. As an English speaker, you can understand a lot of Spanish, French, Italian and Portuguese words simply because they have the same etymology and are written in a similar way as in English.

Can you guess what Spanish *abdomen* means? French *amusant*? Italian *attenzione*? Portuguese *animal*?

If you want to improve your vocabulary, you can get a list of cognates in your target language and learn dozens of new words in a matter of a few hours.

Be aware of false cognates, though. There are some words that sound almost the same, but have a different meaning. One notable example is Spanish *embarazada,* which doesn't mean "embarrassed" but "pregnant." It sounds even more confusing when you say you're *embarazado* as a man.

#4: Improve Your Self-Confidence

The social aspect of speaking in another language is something we can't just sweep under the rug.

When you're learning a new language, you're learning it because you want to understand other people. Yet, so many people avoid speaking a foreign language for as long as possible. It usually has nothing to do with their skills, however. What they lack is self-confidence, the ability to say something in a language they don't know well and not be afraid to make a mistake in front of other people.

If you're shy, don't let it hold you back. Force yourself to step outside your comfort zone and do things that are uncomfortable. In order to learn a new language, you have to try new things. If something related to learning languages is scary for you (say, the mere thought of speaking with a native just a few weeks after you started learning), it's probably exactly what you need.

#5: Get an Online Teacher

If you have money to spare, consider hiring an online teacher. A regular Skype session with a native speaker will help you get used to speaking the language. Moreover, it's much easier to find an online teacher than a pen pal and have regular lessons with him or her.

When looking for a teacher, find someone who focuses on teaching the language using conversational practice. If he or she forces you to learn grammar for one hour, you're going to waste money. Spend each hour training your ear and talking – two activities that yield the best results.

If you're learning a language of a less developed country (say, Mexican Spanish), the rates of an online teacher who is a native speaker will be much lower than you expect.

You can find an online teacher on Italki.com. Some people also advertise their services on Fiverr.com. With the latter site, don't expect to find a professional teacher. However, if you're going to have a one-hour long conversation with a native speaker for five bucks, it's still worth it.

#6: Use Spaced-Repetition Software

If you absolutely can't live without memorizing words in some way, don't use regular word lists – use spaced-repetition software like Anki.

Such programs will help you memorize new words in the most effective way possible, by repeating the words you're having problems with more often than the words that are easy for you to remember.

For the best results, get an app on your phone and practice in every spare moment – when commuting, waiting in a line, waiting for your dinner, basically anytime you have a few minutes when you aren't doing anything.

I've used such software, but in the end I decided it wasn't for me, because it felt too much like studying. No native speaker has learned a language this way, so I figured I didn't need it either. It's your call – try it and see how it works for you.

#7: Think in Your Target Language

Many language learners make the mistake of thinking in their native language even if they're already capable of thinking in another language. Instead of saying something in Spanish, they first think how to say it in English, and then translate it to Spanish, and then say it. This pattern makes it extremely hard to become a fluent speaker. In a real conversation, you can't afford to translate everything in your head before you say it.

When you learn enough words to construct simple sentences in a foreign language, start thinking in your target language. When you want to say in Spanish that the apple is red, don't think, "Okay, apple is *manzana*, red is *rojo*, but I have to say *roja* because it's *la manzana*."

Have a mental picture of what you want to say and use the words in a foreign language right away.

Another technique that will supercharge your results is switching your inner monologue to your target language. It's possible to do it even if you've been learning another language for just a few months. Instead of thinking in English, "I'm out of milk. I need to go to the store to buy it," think this sentence in the language you're studying.

The sooner you stop using your native language as a crutch, the sooner you will become a fluent speaker.

#8: Have a Routine

One of the most effective techniques to ensure rapid progress is to develop a routine and stick to it daily. Learning languages is all about the process, small actions repeated on a daily basis. Therefore, a routine is a must.

To give you an example, you can make a promise to yourself that you will practice your target language for an hour every single day. Don't just say you're going to "practice" the language, though. Pick a specific activity, such as, "I will speak in my target language for one hour every single day."

You can also introduce smaller routines like, "I will learn five new words every single day," or, "I will listen to one 15-minute long podcast every single day." The key is to pick something and stick to it.

Chapter 7: Nine Common Mistakes to Avoid

Every person makes mistakes that slow down his or her progress when learning a new language. In this chapter, we'll talk about the most common mistakes that make it harder for many language learners to improve their skills.

By avoiding these mistakes, you'll greatly shorten your learning curve, as some of these mistakes can affect your progress to a huge extent.

Mistake #1: Laziness

One of the most serious mistakes you can make that will severely affect your progress is learning only one or two hours per week. If you want to learn a new language quickly, you have to make sacrifices and set aside at least a few hours of studying every week, and ideally at least two hours daily.

Most language learners who need years to become fluent in another language learn it only in a class environment. They usually only have a couple classes per week and don't study much outside the classroom.

If an average student has two or three hours of lessons per week, he spends up to 150 hours per year learning a language. If you study one hour per day, or seven hours weekly, you will reach the same number in just five months. Now let's assume you take it extremely seriously and you study two hours per day, fourteen hours a week. Now you will clock your 150 hours in a little over three months.

Does studying two hours per day sound like a lot of work to you? Consider the fact that an average American spends 5 hours per day watching TV[i]. Does studying two hours per day still sound unrealistic to you? If so, perhaps you don't have a strong enough motivation.

Mistake #2: No Diversity

It's easy to get bored when you stick to just one thing. In the previous chapters, I shared with you numerous ways to improve your language skills. Most of them are fun, so they shouldn't bore you.

Don't stick to a bland textbook and don't try to memorize hundreds of words per day, unless you want to get discouraged and slow your progress to a halt.

Mix it up. Spend an hour watching a TV show, read an interesting article, participate in a discussion forum, listen to a podcast. A few activities repeated on a daily basis will ensure you won't get bored so quickly. They will also help you develop your skills in a balanced way.

Mistake #3: Waiting Too Long Before Speaking

Speaking in a foreign language is scary. You are afraid that native speakers won't understand you, that you will say something stupid or that you will misunderstand them.

All these reasons may sound plausible enough to you to avoid speaking in a foreign language for a long time. However, it will dramatically slow down your progress.

I managed to learn Spanish in a few months only because I paid a lot of attention to speaking from the beginning.

The longer you avoid speaking in a foreign language, the scarier it will be to start. Consequently, you should make it one of your goals to start speaking as soon as possible, ideally from day one (even if it's just a few short memorized sentences).

When you get into the habit of speaking in another language right away, you will get valuable feedback from native speakers you would never get from a textbook.

I'm not saying that other skills – writing or reading – aren't important. However, I believe that speaking and listening skills should come before other language skills.

There's a reason for the order of the chapters in this book. Your speaking skills translate to your writing skills, while it doesn't work the other way around.

If you are afraid of speaking in another language, start by speaking to yourself. Record yourself saying something and listen to the recording. You can also upload it to a site for language learners and ask other people to give you some pointers. Feedback from native speakers will make you more confident in your skills, thus helping you get outside your comfort zone and start speaking with other people.

Mistake #4: Not Listening Enough to the Proper Materials

Listening is the key to understanding the spoken language. If you want to learn how to speak with other people, you need to understand what they're saying. It can be tricky if you don't listen enough to the real-world materials.

Many language learners are extremely confused when they listen for the first time to a native speaker talking in a natural way. Language learning materials are usually much easier to understand because they are being read unnaturally slowly.

In order to understand native speakers, you need to focus your time on listening to them speak in a normal way, not in a watered down manner they would never use in a normal conversation.

I have a friend who's learning Dutch. He's been taking classes with a teacher who has been playing him audios for language learners. When my friend met with Dutch people for the first time, he was extremely surprised to discover that he couldn't understand a lot of what they were saying.

It was almost six months after he started learning the language, and he couldn't speak in Dutch with them at all. I'm sure he could be able to carry a conversation with them if he only spent more hours listening to regular content in Dutch, most importantly movies and podcasts.

It's normal that a foreign language feels strange at the beginning. You can't even hear individual words, and it all sounds like gibberish.

But here's an interesting thing – when you stick around and keep listening, your brain will get used to the different pronunciations and intonations. You will start hearing some easy individual words (like "thank you," "goodbye," "hello," and so on).

Later on, you will be able to understand some simple sentences. And then you will develop the ability to extract the meaning from a sentence even if you heard only a few words. This skill will never come from listening to something that's easy. Discomfort is necessary in order to learn quickly.

Mistake #5: Not Paying Attention to Intonation

All languages have a certain tone you need to maintain to sound natural. If you ignore this aspect of a foreign language, native speakers will have a hard time understanding you.

To give you an example, many non-native English speakers have a "flat" sound. Their vowels and consonants may be perfect, but the way they say these sounds is strange. It can lead to many misunderstandings when they forget to stress the right word or use the wrong pitch.

It's the same with every other language. By learning the fundamentals of intonation (which words to stress, how to do it and when your voice should rise or fall down) you will give yourself a solid foundation to build on when speaking and listening to native speakers.

Mistake #6: Not Paying Attention to Pronunciation

Pronunciation is an extremely important part of every language. If you don't know how to pronounce words or individual sounds, you're unable to communicate in another language unless you can write.

You don't have to develop a masterful accent in your first few weeks of learning a foreign language. In fact, it won't happen for a long time. However, you should definitely spend some time learning how to say every individual sound in the language you're learning.

For instance, Spanish vowels are different than English vowels. You can't say *aeropuerto* using the English "ow" sound.

You should take some time to listen to individual sounds (both vowels and consonants) and try to memorize how to say them. You don't have to get them 100% right, though – the goal is to use something that is closer to your target language than using vowels from your native language.

Another important reason for paying attention to pronunciation is that if you teach yourself the correct way of speaking in the beginning, you will have less work to do later, as you won't have to unlearn the incorrect habits.

Learning the Spanish alphabet was the first thing I did before I started learning anything else about Spanish. By learning the vowels, consonants and diphthongs in the beginning, it was much easier for me to listen to the language later and use the correct sounds when speaking.

Mistake #7: Trying to Deconstruct Everything

When you're learning a new language, there's always uncertainty that you won't understand something or that something will be confusing to you. Don't worry about it. You probably have the exact same problems with English, too.

To give you an example, many native English speakers have a hard time understanding when to use "fewer" vs. when to use "less than." If even native speakers have problems with this issue, how do you expect non-native speakers to master this aspect of the language with ease?

It's the same when you're learning a new language. In all languages, there are certain aspects that are confusing to anyone, both native and non-native speakers. It isn't only about grammar, though.

As a native speaker, you sometimes encounter English words you don't recognize. When you're learning a new language, there will always be some words you won't recognize, too. Does it mean you don't speak the other language well? Not at all. There are several hundred thousand words in each language, and nobody knows them all.

When you stop trying to learn everything, you will put an end to the compulsive behavior of checking the dictionary every time you encounter a new word. Instead of checking the dictionary, you should try to understand the word from the context, just like most native speakers do.

If you keep learning the language in a structured and artificial way, you will never reach the kind of fluency native speakers possess. Language is a living thing, and it can't be learned as a list of rules to follow and words to memorize.

Mistake #8: Using Patterns from Your Native Language

Are you looking for a sure-fire way to slow down your progress when learning a new language? Look no further than using patterns from your native language in every aspect of your target language.

Jokes aside, in order to learn a language quickly, you need to completely forget your native language. If you keep using patterns from your native language thinking that all languages sound the same, you'll make it extremely hard for you to master another language.

To give you an example, as an English speaker, you are used to the subject–verb–object (SVO) structure. You say, "She loves him."

Many Asian languages (like Japanese, Tagalog, or Korean) use a different structure – SOV (subject-object-verb). In these languages, you would say, "She him loves."

To give you another example, in English you can put emphasis on a different word and change the entire meaning of a sentence. For instance, "*I* did not steal her purse" has a completely different meaning than, "I did not *steal* her purse." In many languages, you can't use the same approach – it's an English pattern of stressing words.

In order to learn languages quickly, often you need to completely forget about your native language and assume that everything is different. Instead of thinking that if something is being done this way in English, it has to be done in a similar way in another language, just check it.

Mistake #9: Giving Up

I like to say that learning languages is more about your mindset than anything else. If you have empowering beliefs and you're determined to achieve your goal quickly, you will do it. If, on the other hand, you let little frustrations make you so angry that you stop learning, you will struggle.

Learning is a lot about patience and motivation. Don't give up when something is frustrating or confusing. It's a necessary part of the process. When you were learning how to ride a bike, you had to have your share of bruises. It's the same with languages. You need to make a lot of mistakes and experience a lot of frustrations before you achieve your goal.

Chapter 8: Five Common Challenges

There's a whole lot of challenges language learners face when they start learning a new language. In the last chapter of this book, I will share with you five common challenges you may experience on your own journey. I will also give you advice on how to deal with these problems in order to avoid slowing down your progress.

Challenge #1: Being Afraid to Speak with a Native Speaker

Speaking with native speakers is one of the most effective things you can do to learn a foreign language quickly. The sooner you get over your fear and start doing it, the sooner you will become fluent. There's no workaround. Quick results are all about conversational practice.

One thing that helps me get over my fears and speak with native speakers is to never hesitate. Whenever I have an opportunity to practice my skills,

I don't give myself time to think about it. I just do it, because the longer I wait, the scarier it will be.

Secondly, you have to instill in yourself the belief that it's okay to make a fool out of yourself. You have to swallow your pride when you're speaking another language. You're going to make mistakes, you're going to sound ridiculous, and you're going to be misunderstood. All these things are necessary, as they help you learn from your mistakes and improve your skills.

Last but not least, remind yourself of your "why." If you have a powerful motivation why you want to learn another language, it will help you overcome your fear of speaking.

In my case, my motivation to learn Spanish was that I wanted to live in Mexico for a few months. Consequently, whenever I felt afraid to speak with a native speaker, I reminded myself that if I didn't do it, my trip to Mexico wouldn't be as enjoyable as I wanted it to be.

Have your own reason why and use it to fire you up when facing doubt before speaking with a native speaker.

Challenge #2: Struggling with Grammar

For a lot of learners, grammar is the least enjoyable part of learning a language. I agree with this sentiment, especially when you're taught that the only way to learn grammar is to memorize boring rules, verb conjugations, and so on.

In this book, I shared with you ten ways to improve your writing and reading skills. By improving these skills, you will naturally improve your grammar skills.

Keep in mind that sooner or later you will have to learn the rules of grammar, but there's no rule stating you have to memorize them with no reference to the real world.

Writing on a daily basis is the most essential activity to become good at grammar. The more you write, the more often you will try to write something you aren't sure how to write. Consequently, you will check the rules, but only to write correctly what you want to write. When you use grammar in the real world (not in grammar exercises), it's much easier and much more enjoyable to learn it.

Challenge #3: The Inability to Make Out Any Words When Listening to a Native Speaker

This challenge is extremely common among learners who spend their time listening to easy audios recorded for the purpose of learning a language.

When something is easy for you, it's probably a waste of time. Learning languages is about discomfort and constantly raising the bar – just like weightlifting when you constantly have to increase your load to make your muscles grow.

The key to developing your listening skills is to listen to the real-world recordings. The first few days or a few weeks of listening to another language will make your brain melt. However, rest assured that if you keep doing it, you will start making out single words. Later, you will start understanding some simple sentences. Soon, you will be able to understand entire simple conversations.

If you stick to easy audios, it won't happen as soon as when you listen to regular podcasts or watch movies without subtitles. In most languages, native speakers speak much more quickly than the people you can hear on the recording. By getting used to the normal "music" of the language, you will make faster progress than if you were to stick to what's easy.

Challenge #4: Not Having Enough Time to Learn

One of the most common excuses of people who want to learn a new language is that they supposedly don't have time to learn it.

In reality, you can always make the time for an important change in your life. It doesn't matter how busy you are – everyone can find at least a few hours per week to practice a new language. The key is to use small pockets of time you otherwise waste, and to replace your daily activities with the same activities done in your target language.

To give you an example, if you're driving 30 minutes per day, it's 30 minutes you can use to listen to a podcast and work on your listening skills. If you're waiting in a line for 5 minutes, you can open an app on your phone and learn some new vocabulary. When you're waiting for your friend to join you in the café, you can read a page or two of a book.

You can also make a lot of time for language learning by replacing your daily activities with the activities done in your target language. For instance, if you read news on a daily basis, start reading them in another language. If you're watching movies, watch them in a foreign language. If you listen to music while you work, listen to music in the language you're studying. If you love comics, read comics in another language.

Where there's a will, there's a way. If you genuinely want to become fluent in another language, you can always make time to practice it. It's just a matter of your priorities.

Challenge #5: Discouragement

Learning languages isn't easy. It takes a lot of time and a lot of practice to improve your skills and become a fluent speaker. Consequently, many learners give up before they achieve any kind of results.

How do you deal with discouragement when learning languages?

First and foremost, you need to remind yourself of your reason why you're studying. As I mentioned in the first chapter, a strong motivation to learn another language will help you push through obstacles and be persistent.

Secondly, find ways to make learning fun and interesting. It's extremely easy to get discouraged and tired when you're sitting in front of a textbook doing grammar exercises. In this book, I shared with you numerous ways to learn a language while having fun. Use them to avoid feeling burned out.

Thirdly, don't try to be a perfectionist. It's okay not to understand every single rule of grammar or have lacking vocabulary, especially if it's related to something you don't even talk about in your native language. You can always learn the less important things later. In order to avoid discouragement, concentrate on the key things that you will use on a daily basis. The ability to get by in everyday situations is a powerful boost of self-esteem that will fuel you on your journey.

Last but not least, focus on the positives. Remind yourself of the things you already know instead of focusing on the things you don't know or don't understand. This attitude will help you appreciate what you've already learned and keep working on your skills without getting frustrated.

Afterword

Now that you've finished the book, you know some of the most effective tips to learn a new language quickly. Before we part our ways, I want to give you one final piece of advice.

When you're going to start learning a new language, don't give up when you feel frustrated. It's easy to get overwhelmed, especially when you're starting out and you have no idea how the language "works." Remind yourself that it's a process and that frustration is a necessary part of it.

The key to learning languages is to be persistent and take small steps every single day. It requires a lot of patience, but by using the tips I shared with you in the book, it can be quite fun and not as frustrating as sitting in a class with a boring handbook.

Have a strong "why" for learning a language, develop a daily routine, and practice in a fun way. Results will come soon.

Good luck,

Nate

P.S. If you liked my book, would you be so kind as to leave a review? Even just a sentence or two would mean a lot to me, as it would help me reach more readers.

P.P.S. Before I write the last words in this book, I'd like to encourage you to sign up for my newsletter for language learners here: http://eepurl.com/bb8sQ9

As a thank-you gift, you'll get a bonus chapter listing my favorite language learning sites. It's in a .mobi file you can send to your Kindle and in a .pdf file. If you're willing to write reviews, you can also get access to all my incoming titles before I publish them.

Subscribe to My Newsletter

Sign up for my newsletter at http://eepurl.com/bb8sQ9 to get a bonus chapter listing my favorite language learning sites. It's available both in a .mobi file you can send to your Kindle and in a .pdf file.

You'll also get exclusive updates about my new titles. Subscribers of my newsletter who are willing to write reviews have the opportunity to get free advance reader copies of my new books.

Don't worry – I don't send emails more often than once per week (and usually less often than that).

Support the Author

Reviews help authors reach more readers. For self-published authors (like me), they're the lifeblood of the business. Your review – even if it's just a quick sentence or two, means the world to me.

I'd love to read your review of my book wherever you bought it.

Books by Nate Nicholson

I write books for people who want to grow and learn new things every single day. Some of the topics I cover in my books include: introversion, happiness, entrepreneurship and personal growth.

You can access all of my books here: http://www.amazon.com/author/natenicholson.

© Copyright 2015 by Blue Sky Publishing. All rights reserved.

Reproduction in whole or part of this publication without express written consent is strictly prohibited. The author greatly appreciates you taking the time to read his work. Please consider leaving a review wherever you bought the book, or telling your friends about it, to help us spread the word. Thank you for supporting our work.

Effort has been made to ensure that the information in this book is accurate and complete. However, the author and the publisher do not warrant the accuracy of the information, text and graphics contained within the book due to the rapidly changing nature of science, research, known and unknown facts and Internet. The author and the publisher do not hold any responsibility for errors, omissions or contrary interpretation of the subject matter herein. This book is presented solely for motivational and informational purposes only.

---

[i] http://www.nydailynews.com/life-style/average-american-watches-5-hours-tv-day-article-1.1711954

Made in the USA
Coppell, TX
18 April 2023

15752322R00049